RENEWALS 691-4574

DATE DUE

MAY 0 7

Demco, Inc. 38-293

ROMANCE & CAPITALISM AT THE MOVIES

Also by Joan Joffe Hall:

Cutting the Plant

The Rift Zone

The Aerialist's Fall

ROMANCE &
CAPITALISM
at the MOVIES

poems by Joan Joffe Hall

Cover by Judy Ayer Doyle
Photograph by David Morse
Typeset by Parousia Press

Printed in the United States of America

Grateful acknowledgement is made to the following publications in which some of these poems first appeared:
The Beloit Poetry Journal ("Envelope," "For Myself–Age Eight," "Hawk Coming"), *Bloodroot* ("The Frame," "The Sirenians"), *Denver Quarterly* ("Plumb Bob"), *Embers* ("The Balloons," "During the War," "Gradually"), *The Georgia Review* ("The Homeless," "Red Moon"), *The Massachusetts Review* ("No Hanukah Bush," sections 1, 2, 5, "Romance and Capitalism at the Movies"), *The Minnesota Review* ("It's She," "Matthew at Thirteen"), *Pequod* ("Conversations with the Dead"), *The Red Fox Review* ("Midsummer," "World Hunger"), *The Seattle Review* ("The Hawk"), and *Southern Poetry Review* ("Eskimo Print Woman," "Kansas, Sunstruck").

The publication of this book was made possible with support from the Massachusetts Council on the Arts and Humanities, a State agency whose funds are recommended by the Governor and appropriated by the State Legislature; and by a grant from the National Endowment for the Arts in Washington, D.C., a Federal agency.

Library of Congress Catalogue Card Number 84-072705
ISBN: Hard Cover   0-914086-54-5
        Paperback   0-914086-55-3

Alice James Books are published by the Alice James Poetry Cooperative, Inc.

Alice James Books
138 Mt. Auburn Street
Cambridge, Massachusetts 02138

For Matthew and Michael

CONTENTS

ROMANCE AND CAPITALISM AT THE MOVIES

To the child the movie is mysterious.
Like magic, her mother
always knows what will happen. "She slapped
his face," the mother says, "but in the end
they'll get married." Murders—
the child wonders how she knows who did it.
It seems fitting, the mother's like
that with the icebox too, no use
wiping up spilled milk. Does she
have eyes in back of her head? Can she see
into a child's heart?
One day at a school movie some kids whisper
in the row behind. "Just wait,"
a girl says, "that guy's gonna lose his money."
And the child realizes it's not magic,
not her mother, it's movies; if you see
enough of them you can gaze right into
the heroine's heart, her secret love for a brute.
You learn what the everyday fails to teach,
that love goes kiss-slap-kiss,
the filthy rich go broke, and honest
folk end up happy unless they're women
and sacrifice makes them radiant.

RED MOON

It's not that easy on your own.
Ask the girl who smuggles her little sisters

and brother across the border
one at a time under her skirt.

Ask the fat man on a crash diet whose estranged wife
comes home to feed him; ask the wife.

Ask the widow who dreams of her wedding:
she's coming down the aisle in a coffin.

Ask the kid whose divorced daddy
puts her on the bus with a heavy bag.

"Wait for Mommy to come aboard and get the bag."
"I'm big enough," the kid protests.

Ask the woman who feels like a pie in a graph,

the one whose ex-lover complains that the hairs
round her nipple make her look like a witch,

the schoolgirl who comes home to find
her mother cold on the bathroom floor,

the child with a shattered eardrum
who'll say only that she fell,

the woman whose clitoris was cut by a beer bottle
—they are in this for life.

* * *

At the Kollwitz exhibit a student guide tells me
her mother's on unemployment and alcohol;

they don't communicate. She can't go back.
I want what any teacher wants, and more,

their love, to change their lives,
to make the rulers less secure.

We stand together in the gallery
looking down a long track of prints like a view

from the front subway car, an exhilaration
of lines of force and lighted cues:

peasants in the shabby stubble of harvest
and weavers, ready to riot.

Women stand open-handed,
their mouths do not receive nourishment.

In an early etching, "Woman and Dead Child,"
a cave woman, thick knees, hair like mine, mourns.

Smuggle me out, mother, snuggle me in your skirt,
I haven't been there in so long.

* * *

I can't go back either
and this is no case history.

I haven't time to suck on details through a straw,
they demand something.

Will I love the child climbing on my book or head,
or slap it as I do in nightmares

with a razorblade in my hand?
My best friend is worn out

—gold hairs on her wrist still glisten
while she and her child wear the same sullen face.

* * *

When her husband left he said
terrible things, he'd say them of me,

witch, he said, witch; good, let it be said;
witches have their own power,

we get it passing forty.
I was glad he didn't come for comfort:

might I not still find him sexy
with his hair turned to ash?

I haven't time to say what everything means,
just to give evidence, grasping at straws.

In this poem I want to be factual:
I saw the moon rise red tonight.

I shifted gears, turned a corner,
and there she was, rising.

MATTHEW AT THIRTEEN

My son is looking for the right
length of string. He has a big ball
of string ends that he gives me
to hold loosely while he pulls
gently at an end, walking away.
One after another, a dozen
or more strips come loose,
none quite long enough—
his height—for the game
underway in his room.

I've always admired
women with grown sons,
and wondered how a boy's body
finds its size.

            I made
some off-color joke
and laughing he reproved me:
didn't I know mothers
shouldn't carry on like that?
and would I please
not do it in front of his friends.

He told one boy in a fight
about abortion just to imagine
being thirteen, female, raped
and pregnant. The kid refused,
said it couldn't happen to him.
Then don't talk, my son said.

When I call him on the phone
I know I'm hearing my own voice.
When he first got braces

I put my fingers in my soft mouth;
his eyes are mine, his bad skin too.
But also they are his;
and the body lengthens
and hardens, pulls away.

DURING THE WAR

My son comes home from school,
                    swastikas
on his sneakers. "You'd have been in the ovens,"
I tell him, "no matter what.
Scrub those things off.

During the war we scrubbed by hand, used
a bleached stick and the kitchen sink—
who had a machine? Things were old-fashioned
then: down cellar,
stripped to his waist and glaring,
the super shoveled coal. And no dryers.
A hundred feet of rope stretched
from pulleys by upper story windows
to the telephone pole and back:
sheets, towels, clothing flapped
white and colored, fragrant kites flying
out and up and over the heads of us kids.
The very socks led an independent life out there
in my apartment house yard in Brooklyn
and came back smelling of adventure.

The fallen clothespins—
not, mind you, the spring kind I use today
but straight like miniature people—we split
for guns and triggers, the best weapons I,
forbidden guns, could get my hands on
to act out partisan, Nazi, Yank;

while my father, horrified, as if weapons
were just for despots or revolt,
drilled with his hands at the factory cold metal
labeled *bomb bay doors*.

But I was telling you about backyard lines.
We didn't have one. We hauled our stuff
to a clothesline on the roof, my mother
thought it more genteel.
A magic I still dream about lay
in the high metal stair to the roof and the tug
of tar and the breeze in the treetops whispering
among the dowdy clothes my grandpa made us,
A golden land, here we belong.

Below swung the long lines and the lovely
cargo by which we could smell our neighbors'
lives—who had fitted sheets already, and nylons,
and zippers;
              and the telephone pole itself that men
climbed with cleated boots, not our men
but gentiles—look what a knife he takes
to cut the line;
          a pulley
turning in a peaceful screech and
a woman leaning her bosom out,
maybe black arms, the *schwartsa* maid, a class
lower even than our own in this house
of immigrants struggling to rise,
as Debs said, not above our class but with it,

as if with windfall weapons we could sail
from our moorings to the roof
and skirt the basement furnace and the fire
a kid in those days needed courage to get by."

IT'S SHE

Shopping for my mother's groceries I see
several short dark-haired women and each time
think it's she. Until she retired my mother
kept her hair black. From snapshots
at two and four I know my hair was blond,
blond in my family anything less than black,
but from the time I could preen in the mirror
black black black. I dream of being blond,
straight blond hair and I'm the girl next door.
Nowadays I catch sight of it out of the corner
of my eye and I think there's a piece
of cotton or some food stuck, but it's
a gray hair after all—mine. Sometimes in
the sunshine it seems on fire, closest I'll get
to blond. The gray is on top at the part,
flying out rough. When are you going to dye?
my sister-in-law says with her three gray hairs.
I'm thinking red, I lie. When she let it go
my mother didn't look much older. She's
at the beauty parlor, I'm five or six and peek
behind the aquamarine electrolysis curtain,
bad hair, get chased away to the manicures.
All my life I've wanted cold red nailpolish.
Don't want my hair a dead black. No younger.
My grandma's hair was long and even at the end
no grayer than mine now. Each generation
gray earlier. Mother didn't want
Grandma to live with us, get her long hairs
all over, brushing anywhere, bad manners.
Mother brushes right into the toilet.
I help her walk upstairs, the soft skin
above her elbows presses my arm. Her knees
—she can't wear nylons, her ankle's too swollen—
are whiter than in my childhood. Her hair is white.
I am suddenly much too big.

FOR MYSELF—AGE EIGHT

The bead pattern on her brother's playpen
disturbs her; she kicks in the rails.
No creature wants a sibling
yet they all want children.
If she were a stone she wouldn't have babies,
no big belly with people in it
like her grandmother's Russian dolls.
Her mother taught her about sex
when she was five—"every man
has a little woman in him
and vice versa." For a year
she worried how if she wasn't pregnant
she could have a little man inside.
She does not want to be a stone, though.
She prays to read minds
and pitch a perfect game.

Sitting on the floor in knee socks
she builds a block city
to the rug's end: the edge of the world,
although she knows it's round.
She wants to live in that city,
feral and crouching, with matted hair.
She would live forever.
Caught, she wouldn't speak
lest anything she said
be held against her.

She pretends to be Columbus,
but she's no hero, wasn't on the ship
exploding off the coast—
she heard that on the news.

Imagining it at school she becomes
blond and Anglo-Saxon, one of "our boys,"
unlike herself at any rate.

"He never forgot," she writes,
"how his shipmates blew apart. The pieces
whooshed by" like her mother's pneumatic sigh
when she stands up after scrubbing the floor.
It never occurs to her that women are weak.
"He thanked God."

She's afraid to take the story home,
certain her parents will think
she's put her own words in the sailor's head
and not the other way around.
She crosses out the prayer, writes
"he felt lucky." Her parents are atheists,
Jewish atheists, her father says.
They are so proud of her,
they think she's perfect.

She's read that the universe
is infinite; she drifts on a lake
deep as the sky. A strange man
plays guitar on shore,
his eyes poke at her. The lake fills her up,
or she fills it, as she can make her hand a fist,
and that a talking puppet.
She sings along with the guitar, a song
in which, after years on the lake
crouching in a rubber boat,
she bursts the sides,
tumbles out, and swims
like a grownup.

NO HANUKAH BUSH

1.   *No Hanukah Bush*

Jewish women sit around my kitchen,
voices racketing like noisy groggers
that drive away Haman. Not ladylike.
I used to think Hitler
was Haman for our times. If you don't get it
then you get an idea what
it is to grow up among gentiles and not
know their stories, or worse, have to know.
No Hanukah bush, thank you, ersatz cross.
No harangues on Israeli imperialism
unless you're scared too.
In one family evil was making money,
in another, not making.
"We'll make a pretty princess," the nose job
doctor told a third, "out of a monkey."
The fourth woman ran out of Temple on Shabbos
screaming down rainy Brooklyn streets:
"They let us sit with them, big deal,
patriarchs! Covet thy neighbor's wife and donkey!"
With food mothers scold and
in the sick pit of the stomach
teach how to argue,
to sharpen the mind, to weight the heart,
to keep emotion hot at the table
where it's safe.
                    While outside around us
the gentiles keep cool.

2. *Putting Down Roots*

Why have I put down roots
in this soil among tomatoes and azalea
like an oak seedling
only few inches high but striking
deeper than a weed, like Hebrew
with its vowels below—
am I my grandfather at eighty
longing for a garden and a few chickens?
A city would fit better,
a place I could quit
like my old neighborhood,
no real estate
to disguise my true state,
to plunge me into carpentry and cellars
or give me a stake in how the town
runs its schools and lull me
into thinking I'm permanent here
when like any Jew
I must be ready for uprooting
and carry seeds away in my head.

3. *Whose Tribe?*

Let the nose be straight
the hair fine and blond
the eyes not brown
the name not biblical—
and since these are gifts beyond control
let the words come forth
in their native order and inflection
like a colorless stream
from the hard rock of assimilation.

4.   *Cradle*

A baby in my arms, damp bottom
in the crook of my elbow, I fly
torn at the roots
up and down the city until

I'm back at our row house in Queens
outside my parents' bedroom,
the mezuzah painted the green
of the doorframe—invisible.
I smell chicken cooking, hens;
little egg yolks steam in the broth.

Inside my father is singing:
I am a slave and where chains ring
that is my resting place.
The child and I knock.
"So you were an agitator?" I ask.
"Religion," he says, "you can do without.
Politics you've always got."
He pulls down the shades for a meeting.

When I light candles for the dead
I feel my father's hands
cradle my face.

5.   *Four Questions About Surviving*

Were the Jews you aided different
from other Jews? Oh, yes, says one,
our Jews were less pushy.
Like Marranos, some became Christians
for a while and even quit
calling each other brilliant.

In hiding, did they pray?
They lengthened their foreskins,
another says, with bottles,
night after night.
How did the women suffer?
Those we couldn't feed
stopped menstruating.

Did any refuse to be helped?
Some became zombies. One family
that a peasant kicked out in a snowstorm,
says a third, I guided
through a dark forest in which the animals
had become extinct.
We happened upon a man sitting on a stump,
snow almost to his knees; it was
the baker Resnik and he wouldn't budge.
He sat, half-white, half-black, like a tree.
Come, we said, together is safer,
but he wouldn't budge.
He opened his mouth and steam escaped.
As the family trudged on
we looked back and saw him
disappear, flake by flake.

THE BALLOONS

The past crouches in his eye:
his father's electric coffee
grinder high on a counter

in the Stillwell Avenue store,
some refugee cousin muttering
in a chair between the pickle barrel

and a crate of kosher soap.
Now in middle age he could blink
and the event salted away

would tumble out still fresh.
Yet the child in knickers
might be anyone.

His youth too, heated to knife-
point before girls, or learning
cribbage halfway round the world,

is stocked with moments
in which the young man, himself,
moves almost unrecognizable

but for a shared nostalgia:
as when he crossed the pass,
his hair on end in a storm,

and came upon a shepherds' camp
with its flush of whiskey bottles
and a three hundred pound iron

cookstove. His backpack grinding
at his hips, he wondered how
they got it up there.

The past holds still for him,
hangs brilliant in the sky,
a flotilla of balloons loosed

from their individual moorings:
detached and ornamental
the balloons lift so slowly

over the horizon they appear
stationary, like Easter eggs
the size of moons.

THROUGH THE BONES

At the only store open on Labor Day,
ten miles out of town, I bought fish
for my son, just home and newly vegetarian.
I recite his joke—"My Summer Vacation:

a month in Seattle with my father
who studied Buddhism and became a vegetarian
so did I." Last time he saw his father
he announced he wasn't a Marxist anymore.

When he called from Seattle
his voice—like my brother's,
with the faint Jewish inflection I've suppressed—
was as light and Southern as his father's.

The butcher teased the teenage checkout clerks.
Over pegged lobsters and translucent
shrimp the size of bracelets bedded on ice,
I chose a piece of swordfish, thick as filet mignon.

"They keeping you busy up there?" He flapped it
onto the scale. How did he know I taught *up there*?
"Not yet," I said. And he:
"At a thousand a month you ought to be kept busy."

I didn't say "takes a thousand a month to buy
your fish" or "I'm paid twice that and worth it."
My three months off and money to choose
what to eat pinned the words in my mouth.

I drove home mad at the butcher and at my son
who'd sent me ten miles to be insulted. He
feeds me facts: 22 pounds of grain for one of beef,
7 for one of poultry: feed the hungry.

The father tugs at the boy after wrenching
himself away, Christian or Buddhist, ascetic,
apolitical—all that I longed to assimilate
as wide between us as the continent.

In his infancy, after a month of watching him eat,
we turned in bed, each other's faces huge and coarse,
the right size an infant's, our son's face—
and were loosed into love as parents.

As a baby he had legs as tight as drumsticks;
to diaper him we had to force them down.
Now, in October, I cannot hack through the bones
of chickens more like us than any slab of meat.

CONVERSATIONS WITH THE DEAD

The child holds a peanut shell
up to his face
and makes it talk.
"I wish I had a radio
in my mouth," it says,
and he replies
"bring-out-your-dead
bring-out-your-dead."

I've been talking with my own
dead. They say
Do you see this stick, woman?
This stick's been round the world
and still it is only a stick.
I say
stick stick, bone bone
more and more I am a mother
fattening the stick.

They say, eat eat
once we were slaves in the land of Egypt
we feed on our past;
this stick does magic
and still it is only a stick.
Bitter herbs grow on sticks,
sticks are unleavened bread,
stick, we will eat you.

I say, spare my child
no bigger than a peanut,
leave his winter belly
and juicy earlobes,
spare all children.

They say
stick stick, bone bone
good enough to eat,
let him grow round the world
and still he is only a stick.

I say wait, he's growing up
already he's charging me rent on his wisecracks.
Still you are a mother, they say,
eat eat, grow grow
you will not let go
and still you are only a stick.

THE HOMELESS

At a Jewish wedding
the groom smashes a wine glass
under his heel
not as I once thought to signify
the hymen shattered at a stroke
but to recall
amid merrymaking
the destruction of the Temple
and centuries of the Diaspora
ending at barbed wire.

As I paint my house,
focused on the wood grain
under each horizontal
stroke I see refugees
lining documentary footage;
the camera pans quickly
but the faces are endless, alike,
dark; on the horizon
the glare of flames, famine.

This stroke of luck
I learned as a wartime child:
to be born here
and in a small slip of time
while children just like me
were gassed and burned
out of less lucky houses.
I called my left fist Hagar
and tortured it to cry.

I know my house both temporary
and well chosen: in the fireplace
only logs burn.
Once we were slaves in Egypt
my grandfather said,
which meant suffering for others,
subdued rejoicing.

ENVELOPE

1. *My Birthday*

Mid-February. At 7 A.M. the red sun
splits open the birches and thrusts
shadows of pine needles onto the brick
and white living room walls,
the green painting. The leaves
of houseplants—diefenbachia, begonia—
transparent in angled light, celebrate
the sun's daily entrance.

2. *Matthew and Michael*

The first year in this house,
before Matthew was one, I'd wave
his fist into the winter morning.
"Sun," I'd say, wobbling his
fat little shadow, and he'd laugh.

I call Matthew and Michael
to look at the red light
on the walls and warm up
by the woodstove. Only in February
can they see it before they leave
for school: earlier in winter
they're gone by sunrise, later the sun
blinds us at the breakfast table.
"It happens every day," I tell my sons.
"I can pinpoint where it rises
over the roof across the road."
Matt shrugs. He's lived here
his whole boring life, the sun
swinging round all day long.
Michael asks to borrow my gloves.

I tell him about a Filipino woman
I met last week. After forty dark
months in solitary—noon and night
no visitors—she held up a fist
against the dictator.
Now she lives in used clothing
and "new friends' houses."

Clothed in privilege we can barely imagine
her defiance. I bask
in the red light.
My house. My sons.

3.   *Dave and Eli*

Daily I measure my sons' distance
and release them farther. I embrace
new male bodies: a man, his child,
sons of other women. Here they are
coming up the driveway with groceries
and furniture. This whole house
needs stretching.

Each time I dress Eli his head and fists pop
out of the T-shirt. Each time, I relive
my own sons' births, observer
and parturient. No father
shares that pain, but watches
as the odd plum slips out,
then holds his child,
looks down at the arms and knees
of his own father and tightens his hold,
knowing that last year
thirty million children starved.

Dave and Eli wrestle on a mat.
With a plosive sigh as violent
as birth, Eli kicks free.
"Push from the toes,"
his father instructs, and gathers him back
in an embrace.

Yesterday I called Eli
a pet name I use for Michael.
Eli's ribcage
fits warm and fragile with his breathing
under my hand.

4.   *The Architect*

I couldn't tell from the blueprints
how the house would envelope me,
how light would pierce my eyes,
how in calm midsummer the northwest window
would crack open briefly after dinner
with a shaft like sudden guilt
across the kitchen floor.
The house gathers
the sunlight in through south wall glass,
holds it,
exhales a gentle breath.
Slowly I relearn "our."

This change I mark
by writing the architect,
whom I daily praise as the sun
in its orbit celebrates her craft.

5.   *Next Door*

Light bursts and my backyard glows
like a desert test site—
that intense white circle eating up the earth.
What I touch,
what enters my body from the air
or water or the food I eat
shines through my feet in a shoestore X-ray,
my bones as luminous as ribs and veins of plants.
The house is a fragile envelope,
hardly more than the skin
that after years of sunbathing
I now screen from summer sun.

Out my kitchen window
in this suburb of acre lots, fat crows
glut on the compost—
grapefruit seeds especially. Superimposed
upon my neighbor's lawn and its gazebo,
a city backyard spills
with old tubs, a junked Chevy flaking orange;
a frayed rainbow flaps on the clothesline,
a dog whines for meat.
Rats feast in my neighbor's garbage—
she'd buy herself pet food
if food stamps covered it.

I stand behind the glass, snagged
by the glare among the birches.
I call Matthew and Michael to see
where a refugee child lives
in the shelter of a hollow log.
The white circle opens anywhere
—Antarctica, Connecticut.

6. *The Tent*

Should the desolate tent
of the night sky, held up at its peak
by a she-bear, ache
for the huddle of the Milky Way?
Stars, I'm told, push away from each other.
There's Orion, reeling on the hunt,
and Cassiopoeia, raised to her proud throne,
brilliant exiles
in that maypole of constellations empty
as an atom.

I need
food and the warm carapace of affection.
I plan houses snug
in the sunlight, water the begonia,
gaze into the woods. The child,
all rib and hollow eye, returns my stare
saying "Take me in."

OUR LAST WINTER

Our last winter together we stand
afternoons hip to hip at the woodstove,
sometimes swaying in unison like eelgrass
in a stream—though hip to hip's misleading,
my son's four inches taller.
Or we trail each other from kitchen to bath
just as I did with my mother
senior year of high school.
We haven't a clue
to where he'll be this time next year,
what college, what state.
Intensely he courts advice, secures
me to his future, as if he were the stock
and I the graft. Last night I dreamed
he launched himself
from the side of a sturdy boat
into the green Atlantic, striking out
farther than anyone else,
his little brother right behind, who
I feared could not swim. Always I dream
the younger boy is vulnerable, the part
of me apt to sink, in need of rescue,
while I've taught a few essential strokes
to my first born, who has no choice
but to bear me with him.

ESKIMO PRINT WOMAN

She is on the edge of something.
She is inside something.
Her work is local and temporary.

She is the woman who gave birth to a small
monster and nourished it and carried it
everywhere; or she is the monster.

Something is inside;
it does not need to come out.

She is a flying shaman
and her spirits are inside.

When she blows hard
the souls of the dead enter wolves.
When she is cold
the baby in her hood breathes on her neck.

Far out at sea she is rowing
and calling to those on the edge:
she sees them and will survive the journey.

There is a man in the passageway.
There is a bear in the passageway.
Maybe it is a monster.
Maybe she will feed it and keep it close by.

She is the woman who lives in the sun and sees
the whole house inside and out and a whole
day's work all at once.
Her knife is sharp.

Ice flows through her: are her bones
and teeth not white?
She thaws ice into blood.
She walks on ice, her shadow is on the ice,

local and temporary,
but her eyes see to the edge.

WHAT I CAME FOR

I walk out at dawn
through ocean grasses holding down the dunes
to what I've come for—the pulse that beat
all night beyond our bed—and see
the roiling underbelly of the ocean
spend itself in sand.

    In earthquakes
and liquored up I have dizzily thought the earth
turned. Almost I am persuaded
by a jogger's footprint,
toes scalloped deep as bowls,
that the world stands still for clear impressions,
long enough at least for making love.

Menopause frightens me, you said.
It's my menopause, I replied.

    The brew
of horrors that I mull with friends
at home—men and children leaving,
bifocals, gumwork, dysmenorrhea, deaths,
the body sliding out of control—
is tainted with the fear of being unloved.
I hoped the salt air would buoy us
like driftwood leached of sap and resin.

The pull of the outrushing surf at my heel
sucks me down, in, like the weight of blood
or the whorls of shells tumbled
by retreating waves that line by line
invade the wrinkles of the beach.

With gravity, the moon
flirts the ocean from its bed. Losing
my old subjection to the moon I know
the rising tide for what it is, the earth
sliding under the sea.

THE FRAME

The story of his life, he says, and hands
you a small packet of snapshots,
two or three of himself as a child
but mostly his wives and lovers,
one of his mother disconcertingly
like his first wife. When was this?
he asks, as if you've a key.
The women looking out
from the picture frames, ears weighted
with his gifts, seem buoyant.

A month ago you fell into bed
with a guy you'd put up in the study;
you blame the heat for your wandering
through the house that night,
and when he left felt more relieved
than disappointed. Now
he's just a friend, like this man
with the photographs. You rely
on the word "friend" as on a fence.
It's women who slant toward you
from pictures, on the street, at home,
women's voices to which your ears are keyed.

On the back seat of a Studebaker
you and the girl upstairs
acted out fantasies. An older woman
pulled you down to her lap, your breath
stirring the flower pinned
on her blouse. You put your hand
in your roommate's waist-long hair,
the golden horse she called it;
you talked of moving from Cross Street
to Mount Hope, of husbands feeding guns
to children, of a second abortion,

and gave each other a key to life
as if you knew the way around.

You demonstrate ballet, toes
vectoring out. Swing the leg,
you tell her, wheel from the pelvis.

And she tries. You feel her knees
for the turnout; your touch
is professional but her kneecaps
burn your fingers. Later, by the fire,
neatly tucked up, she theorizes.
How did your mother *smell*? you insist,
leaning forward in an awkward lurch
through space that separates you.
You leave fingerprints on her ankles,
earlobes, hair.

In the photograph you mail at Christmas
clear across the continent from Del Mar
you look straight at the camera, your lover
framed by your chair back, both faces subtly
reflected in the windowpane. Barriers
between you and women are transparent
these days, everywhere you look.

GRADUALLY

Gradually he repossesses the apartment:
first the kitchen, tearing down the note
she stuck to the refrigerator: "Ten years,
cook for yourself." He grows small
and cold, nourished on leftovers.
The cupboards empty. The baby downstairs
cries all night; in dreams
he must suckle infants.

He learns how eggs slide in the pan,
yokes tipping into breasts.
He rips out the electric range to buy
an old Glenwood stove with a wood-
burning oven and oils the iron cooking top
till it softens like flesh.
For the first time he knows
he's mortal: this stove will outlive him.

He works in the kitchen, darting out
to change a record or to sleep. The ring
in the toilet bowl becomes his;
the other rooms hover in the doorway,
vast unused space, as if a rib
has been removed, or a beam,
yet the frame still stands.

Last, he faces the bed, strips the sheets;
but for thrift he'd throw them out,
and because he needs to learn
the craft of washing. I'm turning
into a woman, he marvels; then, I'm becoming
a man. Oh God, make me what I could be,
not what I am.

                    Downstairs
the young couple quarrels, he wants
to hug them. He picks up their baby,
wet as it is, and dances it around
through the doorways. Gradually
he can feel the fontanel closing.

KANSAS, SUNSTRUCK

His truck parked at roadside
in late afternoon, the man stares
across the cornfield at a foam of clouds.
The door opens and a child
steps down. She is around eight, blind,
puts her hand on the fender
for balance. Shadows of clouds
race sunshine through the corn.
"Cloud," she says, and "sun."
They practice this game
as if her father made the weather.
When it holds, sunstruck
she presses her other hand
on the metal to gather warmth
and turns her face toward the sun,
ready to fly away. The man
watches like a murre about to plunge
with its chick in first flight
from a cliff overlooking the sea.

PLUMB BOB

He arranges a set of narrow
photographs into a wheel,
points wedged toward the center.
In each his son emerges
from rock split by sunshine,
the boy a plumb bob
suspended in light.

Over and over, one foot poised,
his son strides forward,
no two spokes identical in length;
it's more like measuring a child
against a door jamb, but he feels
the boy is sizing him up.

He cannot now recall
why they separated, he and his son,
but remembers the boy's mouth
fell open at the news. For years
he ached to undo that scene.

A careful look reveals,
hiding in the narrowest wedge,
his own figure. His hat brim
shades his eyes as if the light
would pierce and hurtle him
off its blade.

HAWK COMING

1. *Hawk Coming*

Leaves down, October sun
penetrates the mint bed where blood-
red fingernails of chrysanthemum
arch south. The few zucchinis
and green peppers barely
swell from day to day.
Stuffing my hair in a wool cap
I play tennis early at the high school,
before the yellow buses
roll into their neat formations.
I serve hard to warm my hands.
Some mornings, fog floats on the court
and yesterday a hawk
lay dead on the baselines, feathered
like tweed with angora tufts.
Black people hereabouts say *hawk coming*
meaning winter. I turned it over,
its head wobbled and its body cooled
in my hands. I thought the sky
must have cracked open like ice in a rainbarrel
and the bird, confused by a drop
in temperature, plummeted
through layers of air only to bounce
off the chain link fence onto the court,
while mouse or mole
escaped under the marigolds.

2. *Union Maid*

A wedge of geese flies south, honking,
and ducks hold up traffic.
Inside, at the union meeting

only a few women dare open their mouths.
What did we ever want
that we could name in public unafraid?
I wear a button that says *fifty-nine cents*,
how much women earn for every man's dollar.
Expert at symbolic gesture
some full professors—men—smile.
"Why didn't you sue for a raise?"
"I was feeding five and couldn't risk my job."
At home I reassure my young dog
that birds have a right to use the feeder.

3.   *Cold Frame*

Built a cold frame today:
plexiglass—fifteen dollars,
wood from the old garage,
slope—about thirty degrees.
Nailed it together right above
three tomato plants bearing
heavy green bellies weighted
down to cold dirt.
Transplanted remaining peppers,
tossed chard and the last beans
and eggplant into a stew.
My kids call the stew "soup"
and pick out lumps of beef,
heads hanging over the pot
for a good look
as if they were bobbing for apples.
The world is full of plants,
I tell them; most people don't get meat.
Tonight Orion the hunter hangs in the sky
and I can see my breath.

4.   *Leaf-slick*

In the leaf-slick driveway his bike
jack-knifes like an old pumpkin grin.
My son falls and breaks his right wrist.
We rush to the hospital over back roads
—dogbite, hernia, past emergencies
flash in my eyes. I'm late
to a union meeting.

Wearing a splint like a golf glove
he dictates his math homework in a language
altogether new to me.
I remember the first autumn
the yellowing trees puzzled him.
Like our dog, his whole body
followed the fall of a leaf
—and then another, and over there another—
tracing autumn's accidental grammar.
He needed comfort: *the trees*
won't stay forever bare.

I watch him now, picky meat eater,
left-handed pianist, and write the jargon
of his maturing in his world.

5.   *Sex Roles*

Smartly snapping each garment taut
on the clothesline, where sunshine's down
to a few hours a day, I hang
my husband's jeans and sweatshirt
washed clean of creosote
from chimney-sweeping, a job

he finished that I began ineptly last week.
We're back to old roles.
Fathering, he says, teaches physical risk,
canoeing or crawling in chimneys.
For all I scoff, he splits the wood.
I can't swing an axe
so it lands in the same place twice.

6.   *Cat's Cradle*

Five, six, closeknit
we sit around the table, the only table
of women at the club.
I smell musk: the woman next to me,
once my student and now on her own.
"The other day I looked at my hands
and neither of them had money in it."
The grievance hovers between anger
and sorrow. We lean over coffee cups and papers
as if a cat's cradle string
pulled us into a pattern
for the plot to spin along.
Shuttling between life in a private house
of beds and small bodies
and work at tables like this—so much to do—
I worry that the energy I feel
will hurl me flat.
I draw back and mumble a bitter phrase,
but the knot of despair passes.
Only the ideal is seamless. Speaking
the truth in a gold-leafed courtroom
becomes imaginable. Hands
too long held still, our words now jab or heal
and none of us is on her own.

7. *Time Change*

Now begins the period of darkness.
For a while longer I'll wake to light,
but by late afternoon the dark
drives me cold from windows once bright
toward the core of the house,
toward stove and woodstove.
Often I return home in the middle of the day
to see sunlight
aslant on the living room rug
and smell the salt hay mulch.
The heart booms in the walls
and fertile soil; bitter chard
surviving into winter heralds the daffodils
that bloom year after year.
Our children reach out like tendrils of peas.
I've dreamed that all my family
was in the garden, wearing blue denim,
and I could not tell them apart.

RASPBERRIES

The raspberry must be picked,
you tell me, at the right moment.
It falls into the palm
gently: the lightest touch of a finger
and it loosens,
staining our hands red.

Some of the berries are hardly ripe,
just growing lobes and fuzz, like young girls.
Every day the kid next door
roars by these bushes on his dirt bike
eating Twinkies.

I follow you, cautious and awkward,
through poison ivy and burdock, deeper
into bushes where clusters explode.
You slide behind a wire fence
and hand berries over into a bowl
I've carried out. Some you feed
me direct. Our mouths
and chins and shirts are marked.

Near sunset I notice for the first
time a scar on your upper lip, hidden
under the moustache as if it were a metaphor
for the long-withheld story
of your marriage.
"Like any dumb male," you say, afraid
I'll say it first.

The light darkens
bruising your cheekbones. Trying

to be clear we learn what hurts.
Soon, you promise, we'll gather
the fringed leaves for a healing tea
less bitter than ginseng.

You ask if we can be blood friends.
"That's for people who don't menstruate."
I say; and then you ask if I'd risk
being a blood friend with someone who doesn't.
In that slant light
you could say anything and I
would smile away like any woman in love.

THE SIRENIANS

Acknowledgments:
Delphine Haley, Naturalist
Margaret Randall, Historian

            Returning
to water after eons of absence

the forked legs become a tail, the throat
and tongue learn new hungers and dolphin songs,
skin coats with fur;

              the water
is cold in the Arctic estuaries
where Bering's men caught the sea cow.

Steller, Bering's naturalist,
who also named a jay, noted
that as the sea cow browsed for seaweed
in the shallow waters offshore, placid,
unsuspecting, tail and snout submerged,
it looked like a capsized boat.

Families pastured, keeping an eye
on the "tender little ones." Seagulls
rode their backs to feed on parasites.

Larded up against the chill
by half a foot of fat, inch-thick hide
protected them from scouring by ice
and surf pocked rocks.

The cow was seldom killed
outright; it died lingering as the estuary
tinged with blood.

They were hungry, those sailors,
one can sympathize with them.

Take certain modern victims:
the Chilean revolutionary Lumi Vidella,
tortured every night like her husband
and five-year old son; the man died first,
beaten, starved.

Rats are introduced
into the vagina.
Introduced, introduced: the rat says
Hello, cunt! And the lips of the vulva,
they would purse the word *No*.

Someone slipped Lumi a razor
and she went for the throat of the rapist
who came nightly for all the women;
she was too weak.

He strangled her with his belt
and threw her body over the walls into the garden
of the Italian Consulate,
spotting the grass red.
Other women have written about this;
not all outrage sticks in the throat.

Forty men it took to lug the hooked carcass
onto land. Other sea cows would gather,
slapping up waves to capsize boat, men, machines;
they could not do enough.

The steaks, twenty-five feet of meat,
tasted "exceedingly savory"—we have
Steller's words for it—the fat like almond oil.
The last sea cow was killed in 1768,
killed off for the fur trade.

Naturalists doubt these sirenians
survive their extinction
—though dugong and manatee still swim,
if rare, in warmer waters—
but now and then they are sighted
by Soviet sailors as they toss
whiskered browsing snouts in the air and slap
their forked tails, shifting the gulls.

* * *

As she hiked near Lake Louise and sang
to ward off bears, a woman
saw an elk come dripping out of the water.

Some people have a gift for the rare
and unexpected, the new species. In moments
of terror the edge of extinction cuts
through, and the voice
sings out in rage or hunger or joy.

But hunger is one thing—every baby
eats its mother—and different
from rape or the fur trade. Did the last
dark Steller sea cow see the blow?
Did the grasses, nodding and pulsing
in the estuary, frighten her
or him with a sudden stir?

The estuary bends and forks.
A man is swimming ahead of me
but I can't worry about that now:
I'm giving birth in a pool of blood,
at first on the bed of a shallow inlet
and then on sandy rock.

Young women gather round me, forming a cell,
tender, troubled; but I tell them
not to worry, it's all right.
Boldness increases with numbers
and they begin to sing.

What I suffer, with pain, without pain,
is for the man and also beyond him.

I am giving birth to a dark-haired
child—she is not either of my real sons.
Moonlight reflects off the streams
of sand I kick up, the beach
transformed to a silvery fountain.

WORLD HUNGER

The important things, she tells him, are global:
child care, the environment; they should use
these words as more than slogans,
and look out their windows at the traffic
instead of struggling with each other.

In the morning, after she's cleaned
as much of the kitchen as he can bear,
they go up to the garden. She admires
the zinnias; he picks her a tomato instead.
"World hunger," he says. The tomato's warm
and cool and salty like him. He's suffering
from hay fever and she tries to comfort him
but is afraid of the words he wants—
darling and *passionately*. "I'll give you
what's left over," she says, "after work."

He starts to sing a sea chantey but sneezing
prevents him. One nostril isn't quite clear.
When her babies had colds, she tells him,
she was tempted to lick their noses clean. "Go ahead,"
he says, "lick. Don't you understand about appetite?"
Once he asked Robin to join them in bed—
no threesome; now she says,
"You always catch me off guard. The first time
we made love you lifted me off my feet."
"You're the ant," he laughs, "I'm the grasshopper."

His sexual fantasies frighten her, better
to get it over with at once, now, than risk
getting hurt. "How will it end?" she wants to know.
"You still on the battle of the sexes?"
he teases, "I thought we were concerned

only with revolution."

       While they hoe
potatoes she muses on the end of the world, the sun
growing colder and colder, and no way
to lay anything by.

THE HAWK

Midway in my ascent above the lake
I saw a hawk swoop past to a lower ledge
where it too rested, gray-brown
on a gray-brown boulder, and then feathered
into the foliage.

At every moment you think, Ah, this is life,
this is permanent—rocks
digging shiftily at the sneaker soles,
a step taken in a trill of terror
so that you pitch forward and grab
at a ledge and crawl up
more assured on all fours, and stand erect
to see the hawk, also poised—moments
incised like fingerprints.

But the hawk flies off. The climb,
the doll's house trailer where I slept
for a week, the lake opening warm
to my skin, the loons, those reckless
screamers—all pause only long enough
to be noted and leave me not quite intact,

leave me yearning toward, toward them,
a homesick child, and then away
as the week turns solid and compact,
like a rock skimming across a lake,
spreading calm ripples to the shore.

MIDSUMMER

On a single hook by the back door hang
a cleaver, a fruit-picker like a skeletal hand,
a long strand of rope.
I hear four separate river bird calls
and a blind calf's ignorant knocking
in the barn. Innumerable snuffling creatures
dimple the grass and focus my attention.

I examine a photograph of a slaughtered sow
lying on a platform, white in the sunshine,
and wonder if the men look evil
who shoulder around it, faces obscure.
The picture's called "Singeing: Community Work."
In pauses between kitchen and garden
I rock a neighbor's baby,
the foretaste of a grandchild.

The farm is fat.
At night my husband falls exhausted
into bed, lulled by crickets. Asleep
he takes up little room, curled into childhood,
his large hands still.
I hover in his scent
like the moths who brush the screen, my face
shrouded in a dark tumble of hair,
and feel him twitch as if some life
would knock free of his ribs and flash
like a firefly against the brief night's skin.

As clearly as now I hear the fretful swish
of a speedboat wake chisel the bank,
I can smell the coming cold
and the river rising next spring.

Frogs on the riverbank croak.
Tomatoes ripen into fall. Children as they grow
harden in their skin and at ninety
put their shoes under the bed
for the last time, and for the last stiff time
hang a hat on the hook.

POETRY FROM ALICE JAMES BOOKS